The Current Slavery *in* AFRICA

The Current Slavery *in* AFRICA

Dr. François Adja Assemien

Copyright © Dr. François Adja Assemien.

All rights reserved. No part of this book may be reproduced in any form or by any electronic or mechanical means, including information storage and retrieval systems, without permission in writing from the publisher, except by reviewers, who may quote brief passages in a review.

ISBN: 978-1-64945-391-4   (Paperback Edition)
ISBN: 978-1-64945-392-1   (Hardcover Edition)
ISBN: 978-1-64945-390-7   (E-book Edition)

Some characters and events in this book are fictitious. Any similarity to real persons, living or dead, is coincidental and not intended by the author.

Book Ordering Information

Phone Number: 347-901-4929 or 347-901-4920
Email: info@globalsummithouse.com
Global Summit House
www.globalsummithouse.com

Printed in the United States of America

CONTENTS

Foreword vii

Truth 1 1
Truth 2 3
Truth 3 6
Truth 4 9
Truth 5 12
Truth 6 16
Truth 7 18
Truth 8 20
Truth 9 23
Truth 10 25
Truth 11 27
Truth 12 29
Truth 13 31
    The Rights Of Africans 32
        Article 1 32
        Article 2 33
        Article 3 33
        Article 4 33
        Article 5 33
        Article 6 33

Article 7 34
Article 8 34
Article 9 34
Article 10...34
Article 11...35
Article 12...35
Article 13...35
Article 14...36
Article 15...36
Article 16...36
Article 17...36
Article 18...37
Article 19...37
Article 20...37
Article 21...38
Article 22...38
Article 23...38
Article 24...39
Article 25...39
Article 26...39

Book Summary 41
About The Author 43

FOREWORD

We are in 2020 and slavery officially continues in Africa. In truth, there is no republic and democratic state in Africa. African presidents are slavers. They exploit, oppress and terrorize their peoples. How are they become presidents?

Before 1960, Africa was governed by Europe. This is called colonization. It is the refined form of slavery. In this system, the peoples living in Africa were dispossessed of their civilizations and their goods. They had no right to direct themselves or to produce goods and wealth, to manage them for themselves. They were subjected to hard labor.

From 1960 until today, Africa is ruled by African intellectual elites. This system is called neocolonialism. It is an avatar of colonialism. Its attributes are deceptive and seductive words like independence, republic, Rule of law, sovereignty, democracy, modernity, civilization. Thus colonialism disguised itself in order to be able to keep it for a very long time. To this end, the colonists employed certain Africans to replace them at the head of their colonies. They gave them responsibilities political, economic, social, cultural, religious. These are the official, docile intellectuals they have trained in their schools, their churches and their ideologies. This is how in Africa we have presidents, heads of state, ministers, deputies and black officials. They act and work on behalf of their

Western masters. The power they exercise is colonial or neocolonial power in favor of the West. Thus they cynically develop misery and poverty for their subjects and enrich themselves alone. As great dictators and tyrants, they plunder and waste the goods, the natural wealth, and the raw materials of their country. They sell them to their western bosses. farmers.

African leaders are (omnipotent) Gods. They are the only ones who make the decisions, make laws for themselves and against the peasants. They reduced the African people to silence and to the absolute impression. is there worse slavery? We will present here their criticism made by the outside world, ie the following truths.

BOOK SUMMARY

This book is a moralizing satire. It urges today's Africans to change their character and remake Africa. It pushes Africans to virtue and denounces their most serious faults. It claims a better fate for blacks .

TRUTH 1

> "I don't need to harass you as the French Presidents say France-Africa is over, yet they keep sending you fake tourists who are spying on you and coming back to tell them how to recolonize you".

Let us understand by this that the current tenant of the White House denounces the French neo-colonial policy in Africa. He denounces the hypocrisy, bad faith and lies of the French Presidents. He knows that France does not want to put an end to its colonial action (slavery) in Africa. Indeed, France created its fortune from colonization, which is synonymous with expropriation and cynical exploitation of Africa. France cannot do without Africa because it is poor. It lives only because of the wealth and goods it unfairly and arbitrarily takes from Africa. If it stops doing that, it'll starve. Its population will be unemployed. Its industries will cease to operate. It'll be ruined. It will be its decadence. In order not to be in such a situation, it is doing everything it can to prolong colonization and its imperialism in Africa. It has done so in such a way that its African colonies remain colonies, that it is dependent on them.

No French-speaking African territory is truly independent, autonomous or sovereign. France still has control over all its "old" colonies. It controls them, manages them and exploits their economy as it wishes. It granted them fictitious, misleading, verbal or theoretical independence. In reality, all of them are still at its orders and under its boots. It puts black-skinned governors at the head of these territories (its guarded chases) called lyingly and hypocritically Presidents. The latter are nothing more than its servants and puppets whom it uses as guardians of its interests. It does not hesitate to kill or replace them in the event of treason or disobedience on their part. They could be called "Colonial Slave Presidents". They are very dangerous, harmful, cynical and without any moral scruples towards the African populations. They keep them in slavery and mortal misery by oppressing and exploiting them on behalf of their Master Colonizer and Imperialist (France). They rule dictatorially and autocratically over pseudo-States and pseudo-Republics. There, they change all laws as they see fit and at their convenience, at any time, in the interests of their families and tribes. They change the constitution and electoral code of their countries (at the end of their mandate) to remain in power forever. Without any risk. They have the right to life and death on their subjects (fellow citizens).

In this dog bed, there has never been a fair, honest, transparent, free and credible presidential election. Power is acquired and exercised through army and with the help of France and its imperialist allies, through plots, schemes and arrangements orchestrated by France. It is legitimate and legal through the support and recognition it receives from France and the international geopolitical mafia. The mode of access to power in these colonies is generally coup d'Etat, civil war, genocide and armed rebellion supported, organized and planned skilfully by France (and the West in general). These are the African realities described by President Donald Trump.

TRUTH 2

<< If, after 50 years of independence, you have not built the necessary infrastructure for your people, are you human beings? ».

The American President rightly blames African Presidents who have failed to achieve socio-economic and material development in their countries. Indeed, from 1960 to the present day, African countries have been in dire need of health, school, road and other infrastructure. Their leaders have done nothing significant for them in this regard. This says a lot about the personality of African leaders. This may not be part of their roles and missions (which ones?). In the previous chapter (Truth 1), we presented the global, general, historical and geopolitical context that explains this state of affairs. Western colonialism-neocolonialism and imperialism do not promote the emergence or socio-material and economic development of the African countries they control and exploit. The imperialist West does not seek the happiness of Africans. Rather, it causes their misery, suffering and desolation. It continues to create natural and humanitarian disasters in Africa: drought, famine, disease, poverty, devastating conflicts, wars, armed rebellions, coups and chaos, disorder, economic, political, social, cultural, spiritual and chronic instability. The neo-colonialist and imperialist West likes to fish in troubled waters. It divides Africans to rule over them (Machiavellian cunning and wickedness). It depraved them, alienated them, corrupted them and submitted them to its satanic will. It wants to destroy them and seize all the goods and wealth of Africa. These are its stated ambitions, intentions and objectives. And the terrain is very favourable, clear and free. There is no obstacle against it. Everything succeeds easily, totally and wonderfully. In Africa, everyone is at its disposal and at its devotion. It is seen as the great expected savior or God, the Father. It is pampered, courted and adored. Its schools and churches have put this in everyone's head. These two powerful instruments put African consciences to sleep and produce docile and devoted slaves. African scholars and eminent intellectuals trained by its schools and churches teach everyone that the colonization-slavery of Africans by whites is a great good, a salvation, a happiness, a grace, a necessary evil (see the works of Leopold Sédar Senghor, the works of the philosopher Marcien Towa and so on).

Thus the 50 years of independence have produced bleating sheep and lambs in Africa. The 50 year of independence produced animals and super-colonized animals and not humans. Because the human being is only the one who is reasonable and endowed with historical and moral consciousness (read René Descartes, Hegel and Emmanuel Kant). The human been is conceived as Freedom and Reasonable Will. And thanks to these superior faculties (Reason, Consciousness, Freedom, Will), human been is necessarily virtuous, wise and human-humanist. Human been can never accept servitude, slavery, alienation, oppression, cynical exploitation and colonization (as property). Human been may not constitute a danger or harm to others and his fellow citizens. He must want to be a good patriot and a humanist. Human been necessarily fights historical injustice, arbitrariness and violence, evil in all its forms. Here are, for example, those who have done so in the history of humanity: Martin Luther King, Karl Marx, Nelson Mandela, Jean-Paul Sartre, Jean Jaurès, Jean-Jacques Rousseau, Diderot, Victor Hugo, Montesquieu, Thomas

Sankara, Thomas More, Plato, Socrates, Cicero, Malcolm X, Mahatma Gandhi, Kwame Nkrumah, Ahmed Sékou Touré, Patrice Lumumba, Mouamar Gadhafi, Lenin, Mao Tse Toung, Fidel Castro, among many others. They are the opposite of our current African Presidents. And misfortune dictates that all worthy and responsible African leaders and elites, those who try to do good and properly serve their peoples, be murdered or overthrown. And by whom? By other Africans manipulated, corrupted and used by Western imperialists and neo-colonialists. So what can we do to change the fate of Africans? How can Africa be saved? How can this fundamental African contradiction be resolved? How to get out of this dilemma?

TRUTH 3

"If you sit on gold, diamonds, oil, manganese, uranium... and your people have no food, are you humans? »

President Donald Trump again refers us to the definition of human. Let us repeat: the human being is a being endowed with Consciousness, Reason, Will, Language... Christian theologians affirm that man is created in the image of God (God made man in his image). And God is conceived as a transcendent, omnipotent, omnipresent, omniscient being... As such, he is perfect, pure, reasonable, wise, virtuous. Man is therefore intellectually and morally perfect. He is guided by the Holy Spirit. He is holy. He is incapable of harming others. He is non-egoist, fair, honest, charitable. He knows how to sacrifice himself to others, to give his life to help and save others, that is to say, those who are in suffering and danger. The models of man of this nature are, for example, Jesus Christ, Socrates, Cicero, Thomas More, Thomas Sankara, Mahatma Gandhi, Martin Luther King, Malcolm X... All of them are saints, sages and heroes in ascetic morality, having practiced the supreme virtue of self-giving, self-denial, compassion and empathy to the absolute degree. Their common ideals were justice, good, happiness, the freedom of others. All of them died, murdered, for trying to save their peoples, others and humanity. They wanted a better life, a better world, just and happy for all. Have the African Presidents reached their rank? At this level of Consciousness, Will, Reason and prospective responsibility? No. They do the opposite of their royal duty.

It is in this sense that the philosopher Plato wants philosophers to be kings or kings to be philosophers (see Plato's Republic). Yes, he's right. A political leader must not be a vulgar, ordinary, selfish, unjust, mean, ignorant, dishonest, blatant thief, fieffed liar. For the command function is a sacred, divine function that is suitable only for saints, sages and heroes. Indeed, the purpose of politics is the good of man, the happiness of the people. In this regard, we must read the myth of Plato's cave (in The Republic) as well as Aristotle's "Politics". The function of leader (President, King) is an educational function. Every good leader is an educator of his people, and therefore a model, exemplary, virtuous man. He is filled with wisdom and love for those he commands. He's a perfect servant. He is necessarily good and benevolent. He cannot and must not starve his people. If a President does so, it is because he is not a leader or a human being. The American President is therefore fully justified in considering the so-called African Presidents as unworthy of their office and of humanity (divinity). The latter are ashamed, irresponsible, resigning, incapable and insane. They are absolutely despicable and condemnable. Indeed, Thomas More says in his "Utopia" that "Men have made kings (chiefs, Presidents) for men and not for kings; they have put chiefs at their head to live comfortably free from violence and insult; the king's most sacred duty is to think of the happiness of the people before thinking of his own; as a faithful shepherd, he must devote himself to his flock and lead it to the richest pastures".

The African Presidents are doing the opposite of their sovereign task. They do not think of the happiness of their peoples. And worse, they are their executioners. They are oppressors, persecutors and killers. They are thieves, liars, deceivers, traitors and looters. All the goods and wealth of their countries belong to them in their own right with their Western bosses or masters. They are not accountable to their flocks of peoples. They are sitting on gold, diamonds, oil, manganese, uranium etc. and their people's sheep are hungry. What to do with these fictional Presidents, these actors who only mimic the title and function of President without actually performing it? Africa must get rid of them as soon as possible to be saved.

TRUTH 4

"If, to stay in power, you are not afraid to buy weapons from foreigners to kill your own people, are you men? »

I would like to give my personal testimony here to support this Trumpian truth. I am African, Ivorian. I experienced first-hand the 2010 civil war in Côte d'Ivoire. This war took place because the then Ivorian President, Laurent Gbagbo, did not want to hand over power to the winner of the 2010 presidential election, Allassane Ouattara. As the world asked him to leave power peacefully, honourably and democratically, Mr. Laurent Gbagbo preferred to wage war in order to remain in power. He had several thousand people massacred (Ivorians and foreigners, innocent women and children). He spent billions of CFA francs to buy weapons from abroad to wage this despicable and unjust war. He said out loud, proudly and cynically (with a disconcerting lightness): "If you want to take me out of power, I will give ten years of war to Côte d'Ivoire". Thing said and done. This case is, unfortunately, general in Africa. All our African Presidents maintain power through military force, barbaric, savage violence, carnage, genocide, arbitrariness and cynicism. This means that for them, the lives of their fellow citizens have no value. Human life is nothing. Moreover, they have the right to life and death on all those who live in their countries. Everyone is choreable and can be cut at will. As in Europe of yesteryear, under kings.

The theory of Human and Citizens' Rights (proclaimed by the UN in 1948) is not respected or applied by any of our African Presidents. Almost all of our Presidents are cannibals and vampires. They kill and eat the flesh of their fellow citizens and drink their blood. It is the means (their golden rule) by which they acquire, it is said, the magical-mystical power they need to exercise power effectively. They take ritual and mystical baths with the blood of their human victims in order to consolidate and eternalize their power, in order to increase their power and influence on the world. Political greed, selfishness, megalomania, egocentrism and mystical-religious superstition are essential. Poor Africa! Poor Africans! For these practices of enchantment and domination, priests, pastors, Imams, marabouts, charlatans, wizards and other gurus or spiritual masters are present in the presidential palaces. They are rushing and are at the devotion of the Presidents who are too eager for power, success and popularity. They are paid very high prices, with billions of cfa francs. For their dirty work of human sacrifice and so many other odious and criminal things. Africa is sick of it. Really very sick. Africa is sick of its millions of children who lack Reason, Consciousness and humanity. Africa suffers too much from the defects, vices, nonsense and filth of its children, which can be likened to animals and things. The American President is absolutely right to judge Africans as he judges them. In doing so, he is very honest, truthful and humane. He pities Africans. He's condescending. He feels sorry for us. He mourns us. Africa is a real garbage can, a huge dump (shit hole) housing monsters, witches, savages and barbarians ignoring all the good manners, values, good habits and good models of universal modernity: democracy, republic, rule of law, Human and Citizens' Rights, humanism, ethics, morality.

Africa is a continent currently populated by people who are against progress, development, emergence, good, happiness, good health, prosperity, success, etc. Africans imprison and kill their own people instead congeners who desire the good, progress and happiness of all. They love and adore their worst enemies or Presidents who buy weapons to slaughter them. They love those who starve them, who import toxic waste from abroad to poison them and kill them massively in order to get richer (the scandal of the ship called Probo Koala in Côte d'Ivoire under the regime of President Laurent Gbagbo considered as socialist). Africans prefer criminals, their bloody dictators, thieves and looters (who ruin their countries) to honest people. They are very naive, too easy to deceive, corrupt, manipulate and seduce like babies. They are uncritical. They never hold their unjust, dishonest and murderous Presidents accountable. To do so is to commit sacrilege. Indeed, African Presidents are considered sacred beings. They are Gods.

In Africa, competition in evil is being instituted. Champions in difficulty are very well appreciated and very well rewarded. Only evil pays very well in Africa. The property is prohibited. Doing good is wrong. The executioners of the people are praised, decorated, worshipped, glorified and congratulated. Crooked and criminal politicians enjoy total impunity. They are above legal, moral and religious law. Indeed, they are the law. They are free to do whatever they want. They are not judged, criticized or worried. They happily do the number of years they want in power (several decades). Only their natural death can remove them from power. They break all world records for longevity in power and all world records for crime (political crimes, economic crimes, social crimes, cultural crimes, blood crimes).

TRUTH 5

> "If your only social project is to remain in power for life, are you human?"

This truth contains five negations: negation of the State, negation of politics, negation of the republic, negation of the function of president, negation of the human (humanity). Remaining in power for life (and especially without giving anything to the people) is not a republican, state, political, human, social value or an attribute of the office of president. This is anti-republican, anti-presidentialist, anti-state, anti-political and anti-human in the context of political modernity. And that, unfortunately, is the general characteristic of our African Presidents.

In the ideas of politics, republic, state, human, president and social project are inscribed the good, the common good or general interest, that is to say the happiness, well-being and salvation of the people. Indeed, politics consists in promoting the well-being or happiness of peoples. Politics has that in its definition and in its substance or essence (see Aristotle in "The Politics"). Politics is essentially and absolutely a moral and humanitarian activity because it consists in doing good. It is not the art of harming or mistreating men. It is humanism and humanitarianism. Remember the text by Thomas

More that was inserted in this book (Truth 3). Also remember the myth of Plato's cave on the function of the king (see The Republic) mentioned in the same book (Truth 3). A politician who does not embody the ideal of good luck is not a politician. A President who does not possess this virtue (to do good and give happiness to the people) is not a President.

The republic (res publica in Latin meaning the public thing or the common good) is precisely the instrument that makes it possible to realize the most beautiful dreams of peoples, to best satisfy all the needs of men living together in civil society: freedom, justice, prosperity, equality of rights, duties, peace, happiness, progress... You are not President for yourself and for your family. Unfortunately, this is what is happening in Africa. For there is no State as the government of man by just, egalitarian law as an expression of the general will. There is no republic, no politics, no democracy ("government of the people by the people and for the people") and no humanism-humanitarianism. It is very sad and very serious. President Donald Trump saw this. The fact is there. It is undeniable. The African peoples are suffering atrociously. They are very unhappy. African young men and girls are desperate. They flee their continent. They are going to the West. At the cost of their life. That is a general disaster. African presidents are insensitive, cruel and absolutely incapable of feeding, housing, caring, educating, defending and securing their populations. They are totally unable to create jobs for them, to provide them with clean water and electricity. They are absolutely unable to build roads, bridges and factories to employ young people. That is the general distress.

African peoples are left to their own devices, to their own plight and to misery, poverty, unemployment, sickness and death. This is the situation in Africa with its Presidents for life without vision, without a social project and totally irresponsible. It is sad, alarming and revolting. Thank you, President Trump, for denouncing this (all these defects and crimes). You are our mirror. You allow us to see and know each other truly as we are. We are ugly, dirty (morally), beasts and wicked to ourselves (shit hole). We are against ourselves, against our own interests. Our continent is a land of all paradoxes, all contradictions, all evils and all nonsense. We Africans are ashamed. We are the laughing stock of the whole world. I fled Africa because of its crimes against humanity and its failure to respect human rights. It's really hellish. As an eyewitness, I have experienced very horrible and indescribable things. I survived by miracles. I was able to escape massacres by miracles. My fate is the fate of all committed writers and thinkers, humanists and activists. As soon as you allow yourself to denounce the crimes and misdeeds of our African leaders, you are signing your de facto death warrant. You are persecuted and sentenced to death. Criticism is prohibited. And that's what I do. You should see my books entitled: "The African Rebels", "The Banned Ivory Coast", "Electoral Code", "The Eleven Evils of Côte d'Ivoire, Countries at War", "Afrocratism", "Political Thinking to Save Côte d'Ivoire", "Côte d'Ivoire with its Foreigners"...

Our African situation is totally absurd and unacceptable everywhere else. We must at least have the courage (and honesty) to recognize that, to be aware of it and to have the will to change, to correct ourselves and to progress towards good and happiness. Our case is not inevitable. Our current situation can improve if we become fully aware of it and want to change. If we decide to change. To want is to act and it is to be able. To want is to think well, and to do well. We really and absolutely need to change our condition in the world. We totally lack a sense of dignity, a sense of duty, a sense of honour and a sense of responsibility. We Africans must emerge from our torpor, our lethargy, our indolence, our carelessness, our superstitions, our illusions. We must abandon our cowardice, our fear, our ignorance, our laziness, our taste for ease, our naivety and our false hope that Westerners and Asians (foreigners) will save us and do everything for us, in our place. For centuries, we have been so with too many serious and deadly defects. This has favoured our slavery and colonization by the West and the Arab world. We must wake up now and fight to meet the challenges of independence, autonomy, sovereignty, freedom, development, justice, prosperity, emergence and happiness. We must fight to death, work, create, invent our future and create our new bright, glorious and healthy history. Thank you, President Trump, for whipping us to make us think and philosophize. The Akans of Côte d'Ivoire say in proverb: "If someone puts pepper juice in your eyes, you have to thank him because he helps you see more clearly".

TRUTH 6

"If you despise and shoot your own citizens like game, who will respect them? »

Yes, African presidents despise, kill and massacre their citizens, whom they consider to be their slaves or objects. They deny them all humanity, dignity and value. So they practice all kinds of wickedness and cruelty against them. They are cynical and sadistic towards them. They have no respect for them. They give themselves the right to life and the right to death over them. They think they have no duty towards them. So do we, Africans, have a duty to consider these ruthless executioners as Presidents (our Presidents)? In Africa, we are neither in republics nor in states of law nor in democracy. We are in a society where political power is personalized, individualized, tribalized, autocratic and absolute. Our absolutist and totalitarian leaders believe that they are of a different and superior essence in relation to their subjects. They believe their mission is to crush and oppress only their subjects. This is their only sovereign duty. They are seeking foreign assistance to accomplish this macabre task.

Our Presidents do not ask anyone to respect their slaves of citizens whom they themselves despise, oppress, persecute and massacre as they want. Instead, they would wage war on anyone who would defend their victims, criticize, disown and condemn their policy. They do not accept lessons from others or blames. Africa is thus a real jungle. For all these reasons, Africans are not respected in the world. Nowhere. They are despised, tortured, persecuted, oppressed and exploited as things, slaves and animals. They are killed and sold in the Maghreb, Arabia, China, India, Asia, Europe, America and elsewhere with impunity. Yes, with impunity. I mean with impunity. They are helpless in Africa, at home, and elsewhere. It's very serious. Too serious. What a sad fate! What a shame! The whole world has, so to speak, the right to life and death over Africans who, however, feed and enrich everyone. What a paradox! What nonsense! What a dilemma! We Africans, Blacks, are always and eternally victims of racism, colonialism, neo-colonialism, slavery, neo-slavery and imperialist prejudices and plots that are perennial. Victims from all over the world. What a tragedy! We remain the eternal damned of the earth! Frantz Fanon is right.

TRUTH 7

"The worst thing in Africa is that if you try to talk about what's right, they'll beat you, imprison you or make you disappear."

Yes, we don't like good citizens or good in Africa. It is rather evil that is loved. Our leaders terribly hate truth, justice and those who criticize them and denounce their bad actions. They're mad at them to death. They take criticism as a lese-majesty crime. It is strictly forbidden. No one will understand and support you if you dare to challenge harmful government action or oppose illegitimate, cynical and arbitrary power. We Africans are educated to be sheep and to accept all unjust and harmful government actions and decisions. In our countries, in Africa, political authority is considered sacred. Whatever it is and whatever it does wrong, it is absolutely respected. And the duty of the citizens-slaves-sheep is to obey power blindly. To criticize power is to sign one's own death warrant. It means exposing oneself to arrest, torture, incarceration and killing. Democracy, human rights and republic do not exist in Africa. These ideals and values are not made for Africa where we adore leaders, whoever they may be. Thus it is not allowed to dream, to think freely and to have personal opinions or opinions contrary to those of our Presidents. If you dare do that, you will be seen as a madman, a suicidal. Thus, during 58 years of independence, Africa has not evolved positively. It always dislikes truth, justice and freedom that allow society to progress, to develop, to be prosperous, rich and powerful. And that's really the worst thing about Africa. We don't have wisdom. We kill all those who tell the truth, demand justice, good, happiness and salvation from all. This murderous, stupid and unpatriotic policy has unfortunately claimed too many victims. And the list of its victims (martyrs) continues to grow. Some famous names can be mentioned here: Thomas Sankara, Ahmed Sekou Touré, Kwame Nkrumah, Patrice Lumumba, Mouamar Gaddafi, amilcar Cabral. Scientists such as Sheikh Anta Diop and Joseph Ki-Zerbo were not heard. Instead, they were persecuted until their death. Too bad for Africa! Woe to any society that persecutes or kills its philosophers.

TRUTH 8

"Blacks sing and applaud their corrupt leaders. They worship their outrageous religious leaders as if they were gods. So who denies that the nigger was born a beggar, grows up as a beggar, gets sick as a beggar and dies as a beggar? »

Yes, everything is overturned in Africa. The abnormal became normal and the normal became abnormal. This means that Africans are totally insane. They do the opposite of things. They take evil for their own good. They consider dishonest politicians and religious as their heroes, role models and gods. They sing their praises, glorify them, magnify them and worship them. They admire them and imitate them as their landmarks. Thus every African aspires to be very dishonest (bandit, villain and dangerous). It is an emulation, a general competition in evil. A macabre general competition. It is a very serious collective disease. No one is normal or sane. The appreciative gaze is totally reversed in Africa. Anti-values have taken the place of values. Corrupt leaders are congratulated and praised. What world then? Where have we seen this if not in Africa alone? Everywhere else (where people are normal, sane, not sick), dishonest and evil people are hated and punished. They are condemned. They are fought with all the strength and rigour of legal, moral and religious law. They are not happy, free and at peace. They are not seen as role models, heroes to be imitated. They are not admirable, loved, adored. In this way, the societal order is maintained with rigour and justice is preserved to guarantee security, well-being, harmony, peace and happiness for all. No one can be above the law. Presidents, ministers and all other citizens are equal before the courts and the law. This is the principle of the rule of law, the republic, democracy (equality of opportunity and condition). All men are born free, equal in right and dignity. The legal law is made by everyone and for everyone. It serves and controls everyone. It is used to judge and fairly sanction the actions of each person. This is the rule and this is the reality in any developed and civilized country. This is the main principle of modernity in force in the world.

Religious leaders (pastors, priests, marabouts, imams, gurus, popes) are required to respect and apply (and to enforce and apply) legal laws and divine commandments. But in Africa, they are not just, honest or holy. They are worse than unbelievers and their faithful sheep. They cheerfully, without blinking, violate all human and divine laws. They are the real devils and demons they claim to be fighting. They are more dangerous and harmful (since they are real and concrete) than satan, devil and abstract, mythical, mythological and illusory demons such as religious fictions, dogmas and lies. They bewitch, seduce, deceive, steal and swindle their herds with their rhetoric and magic. They betray the spirit and letter of their so-called divine mission. The stupidity is at its height in Africa. No serious business. Nothing correct. Nothing reasonable. Nothing fair. Nothing good. Too many contradictions. Too much nonsense. Too many paradoxes. Impenitent criminals who rule Africa. Impenitent sinners who teach divine morality to people. What bad faith! What hypocrisy! What a ridiculous thing to say! What a shame! What a diabolical thing! What a macabre face!

Begging was born and grew up in this infernal context. It thrives on infinite crimes and sins. As long as we Africans do not change, we will be beggars forever. As long as we do not understand that we have rights to claim with our political and religious leaders, we will always be their SHEEPS of sacrifice. There is no virtue and salvation in resignation to crooked politicians and religious. Virtue and salvation lie rather in the ability to revolt one day, to protest against our dishonest political and religious leaders. Virtue consists in wanting to change everything. Africa is now too weird. That's the least we can say about Africa. Let's make Africa better. It is imperative. Let us be serious patriots and revolutionary humanists. Let us have our Martin Luther King, our Malcolm X, our Lenin, our Mao Tse Toung, our Fidel Castro... Let us have others Thomas Sankara, Sekou Touré, Kwame Nkrumah, Mouamar Kadhafi, Patrice Lumumba, Amilcar Cabral, Haïlé Selassié... Our future, which I wish glorious and bright, is at this price. Young PANAFRICANISTS, you are Africa's hope and future. Fight as hard as you can to change Africa's destiny. Fight properly to take power in Africa. History calls you to patriotic duty. Let us stop being bleating sheep or lambs and beggars in Africa and elsewhere. Let us stop being eternal slaves. Let us stop being pitiful in the world. The strength is on our side. It's not in our enemies' house. Let us use it through revolutionary action, through our total mobilization, through our courage, through our perfect union and through our active solidarity against the unjust, criminal and unacceptable order in Africa. Let's change Africa!

TRUTH 9

"The black race is a creature that lacks long-term vision. A black person is stupid because he can't plan his life for more than a year. How can a black man claim to live well without planning his life? »

We want happiness, success, prosperity, wealth... To achieve that, we must work methodically on our lives. We have to heal, order, plan our life. It is a scientific and strategic work. We have to think and calculate our life by submitting it to a master, technical plan. This plan, which contains projects to be carried out in the short, medium and long term, must be strictly followed. This is called living rationally. It is the work of Reason, of intelligence. We got do our best to avoid misery, poverty, suffering and misfortune. We need to be at peace, in harmony, in balance. We need to avoid precariousness, economic and social instability. That is what economics or domestic life sciences are made for.

At the country level, this work is the responsibility of the government. We need a planning ministry. Is there any in our African countries? If so, is it functional, effective? Because we know that nothing is being done seriously or honestly in Africa. Since everyone is cheating and corruptible. The rulers steal and misappropriate all the country's property and wealth (mismanagement). They totally neglect their duties and their work. Thus, any national activity is automatically doomed to failure. And this is chronic. Corruption, negligence, mismanagement, impunity, selfishness, malice, disorder, and irresponsibility spoil everything. These defects explain all the misfortunes in Africa.

Individual and collective life planning is essential for happiness. It is a healthy virtue. We need to do that seriously and effectively in Africa. The bright future of the entire continent depends on it. Thank you, President Donald Trump, for bringing this vital thing to our attention. God bless you!

TRUTH 10

"Give the Negro money for development and he starts practicing witchcraft, hating, killing".

Yes, our African leaders receive money (a lot of money since the beginning) from the West in the form of loans or development aid for their countries. But what do they do with it? From 1960 to the present day, what have they been able to do that is good, concrete and significant for their countries with this money? Is there development or a simple emergence in Africa? Are African peoples living well? Are they happy? Are they saved or lifted out of poverty, misery and precariousness? Can they be compared to the European, American and Asian peoples (without natural resources)? Is there clean water, electricity, paved roads, schools, hospitals, abundant food, medicines, doctors, teachers, factories, industries in our African countries? Especially in our countryside or villages? Is there any job for young people? No. What is the purpose of the money given by the foreigner? Nothing useful for the people. It is wasted and misused. This money is used for futile, personal purposes. It is used to harm. It is used to buy weapons to kill innocent Africans, to wage wars of power retention, to subdue, dominate and crush subjugated slaves. The money borrowed or received as a gift allows the leaders to live in insolent, bourgeois (wasted) opulence. This money makes them and their families richer. The rulers send some of this money back to Western (Swiss) foreign banks, buy castles and other very valuable goods in the West. It's really madness and witchcraft. Because it's malfeasance. It's stupid and absurd.

Our leaders are totally devoid of logic, common sense and reason. They have no human, moral, patriotic or civic sense. They do not seek and do not want the good and happiness of their peoples, but rather their misfortunes. They are Africa's worst enemies. Their essential role is to get richer, mistreat and massacre their peoples. The more they shed the blood of their fellow country men's slaves, the happier, proud and satisfied they are (shame and scandal). It's witchcraft. They are all witches and vampires. They do not deserve the prestigious and honourable title of President of Republic. This glorious title is usurped. It is nonsense. A deadly contradiction. And what republic are we talking about? Can this shit be called a republic? (shit hole). There is no President, no republic in Africa. There are only colonies like gigantic Prisons in which Blacks are enslaved and commodified. And they are starved, mistreated and slaughtered every day. Infinite genocides accompanied by diseases of chemical origin (AIDS, Ebola, Covid-19 etc.) throughout the continent. The objective of the settlers with their black employees and accomplices (Presidents) is the systematic planned (skillfully) extermination of all Negroes, the extinction of the black race. Because of the infinite riches that are in Africa. They are driven by greed, jealousy, selfishness and the instinct for domination.

TRUTH 11

"Even a stupid idiot knows that Blacks don't know what they want."

Blacks don't want anything good. They want one thing and the opposite thing. They don't know what they want. It is absurd and totally stupid. Insane. Is it finally a curse to be a Black? Is it a mortal sin? What did the Blacks do to the God of Christians and Muslims who is making them suffer such a fate? Priests, Pastors and Imams, I beg you to answer me. I'm not normally superstitious. But here, I feel compelled to be. Situation is the law. We Blacks don't know how to separate right from wrong. We became blind and deaf. We confuse everything. We have lost Reason, intelligence and memory that separate man from animal, plant, stone, water, gas and wind. Why? Why? Because Blacks kill Blacks. No regrets. Africans are constantly wronging, hurting and betraying each other.

Africans or black presidents massacre their peoples, slaves, choke them, squander and sell the wealth of their countries to foreigners. They are totally destroying their countries. However, they advocate peace, freedom, justice, happiness and development. They have even developed a very important text entitled "African Charter on Human and Peoples' Rights" (we will see it later). They always talk about peace. But they're still at war. They preach justice. But they practice injustice and arbitrariness. They talk about freedom, democracy. But they are all inveterate dictators. That is the height of ridicule. They talk about republic but they are very authoritarian autocrats. They talk about socialism and communism. But they are cynical, sadistic and immoral capitalists. They say they love the day (light). But they always walk in the dark (in the night). They claim to be telling the truth to their peoples. But they only lie and tell falsehoods and untruth to the latter. They claim to be honest but all they do is cheat and deceive the world. They say they want to feed their populations abundantly while they starve them to death. All in all, they present themselves as angels but they are, in reality, devils. They are all actors and jokers. That is the fair of bad faith and demagoguery.

TRUTH 12

"You all know that Blacks don't know how to govern themselves. Give them weapons and they kill each other."

These are Blacks from the post-colonial period, the period of Presidents and Republics in Africa. The African countries that have become supposedly independent do not know how to govern themselves. From 1960 to the present day, the situation in these countries has been very deplorable and critical at all levels: political, economic, social, cultural, spiritual...

At the political level, it is a general disaster: dictatorship, autocracy, despotism, anarchy, imbroglio. We have gone from bloody coups d'Etat to civil wars, armed rebellions and terrorism. There is widespread instability. The disastrous consequences are violence, insecurity, disorder, infinite suffering and popular misery.

Economically, it is widespread poverty and begging. It is the policy of reaching out to the West to loot, steal and confiscate all our property and immense natural resources.

In social terms, it is chronic unemployment, lack of employment, lack of schools, hospitals, roads, drinking water and electricity. It's famine, disease and death. No well-being. The populations are very unhappy. They languish pitifully in total suffering and misery. It's dramatic. People are killing each other. Tensions, conflicts and barbaric violence everywhere (genocides). Catastrophic governance. All evils pass through it: corruption, mismanagement, clientelism, tribalism, nepotism, selfishness, egocentrism... All this under the diabolical instigation of Western neo-colonialism and imperialism. God made us kings, but unfortunately we prefer to be slaves. God has offered us a paradise (Africa) but, alas, we have transformed it into hell. By our cruel lack of wisdom. Too bad for us! Very unfortunate!

TRUTH 13

"The white man was cultivated to lead the black man. Africans spend their lives dreaming awake".

It is obvious. It is reality today. It's irrefutable. Whether it pleases those who refuse to face reality (case of schizophrenia). That is not racism. The white man totally succeeded. Slavery, colonization and neo-colonization of Blacks are eloquent examples of that. If God created the world, the white man recreated it in his own way, according to his taste, his power and his interests. And he controls it perfectly. He governs and dominates the entire universe. The white man has been able to set up a global system, absolutely powerful and effective, which allows him to always direct and dominate the black man, his pupil and his slave (except perhaps the black man of the Pharaoh era). The White remains the Master and possessor of Africa. He is the real, living and incarnate God whom the Black worships. The African is his big baby, his thing and his private property. As long as the Africans continue to sleep, to be unconscious, irresponsible, incapable, cowardly and stupid, it will be so. As long as they still want to be subjected to foreign domination and do nothing to change their fate and situation in the world and in history, it will be so. As long as they continue to accept geopolitics and the white system of world domination, it will be so. As long as they continue to take evil for good, the white man for their God and their expected savior, it will be so. As long as they continue to proudly bless and glorify white models (political model, socio-economic model, model of society, model of culture, civilization, thought, it will be so.

To say that is not to be pessimistic or defeatist but rather to be realistic, objective and truthful. All obstacles to freedom, peace, happiness and salvation can be overcome. But only if you WANT to overcome them. To want is to be able. No fatality. President Donald Trump wanted to be President of the United States of America and he became President. The Master is Master because he wanted to be Master. The slave (or the colonized man) is a slave because he wanted to be a slave. President Donald Trump is challenging Africans by telling these truths that I am commenting on, and it is up to us Africans to want to take up this titanic and historic challenge. Let us be Spartacus of ancient Rome. Our freedom, our dignity, our prosperity, our happiness, our greatness, our power and all our future depend on it. Thank you, dear President Trump.

THE RIGHTS OF AFRICANS

At the height of ridicule, scandal, hypocrisy and bad faith, the African Heads of State, members of the OAU, have drawn up a very important document (paradoxical to their actions) entitled: "African Charter on Human and Peoples' Rights". Here is a very funny extract. "Hell is paved with good intentions." That's a really macabre grimace.

ARTICLE 1

The Member States of the Organization of African Unity, parties to this Charter, recognize the rights, duties and freedoms set forth in this Charter and undertake to adopt legislative or other measures to implement them.

ARTICLE 2

Everyone is entitled to the enjoyment of the rights and freedoms set forth and guaranteed in this Charter without distinction of any kind, such as race, ethnicity, color, sex, language, religion, political or other opinion, national or social origin, property, birth or other status.

ARTICLE 3

1. All persons enjoy full equality before the law.
2. All persons are entitled to equal protection of the law.

ARTICLE 4

The human person is inviolable. Every human being has the right to respect for his life and to the physical and moral integrity of his person. No one may be arbitrarily deprived of this rights.

ARTICLE 5

Every individual has the right to respect for the inherent dignity of the human person and to recognition as a person before the law. All forms of exploitation and degradation of man, including slavery, trafficking in persons, physical or moral torture and cruel, inhuman or degrading treatment or punishment, are prohibited.

ARTICLE 6

Everyone has the right to liberty and security of the person. No one may be deprived of his liberty except for reasons and under conditions previously defined by law; in particular, no one may be arbitrarily arrested or detained.

ARTICLE 7

1. Everyone has the right to have his case heard. This right includes:
    (a) the right to bring before the competent national courts any act violating the fundamental rights recognised and guaranteed by the conventions, laws, regulations and customs in force;
    (b) the right to be presumed innocent until proven guilty by a competent court;
    (c) the right to a defence, including the right to be assisted by counsel of his or her choice;
    (d) the right to be tried within a reasonable time by an impartial court.
2. No one may be convicted of an act or omission that did not constitute, at the time it occurred, a legally punishable offence. No penalty may be imposed if it was not foreseen at the time the offence was committed. The sentence is personal and only affects the offender.

ARTICLE 8

Freedom of conscience, profession and free practice of religion are guaranteed. Subject to public policy, no one may be subjected to coercive measures designed to restrict the exercise of these freedoms.

ARTICLE 9

1. Everyone has the right to information
2. Everyone has the right to express and disseminate their opinions within the framework of laws and regulations.

ARTICLE 10

1. Everyone has the right freely to form associations with others, subject to compliance with the rules laid down by law.

2. No one may be obliged to belong to an association subject to the obligation of solidarity provided for in Article 29.

ARTICLE 11

Everyone has the right to assemble freely with others. This right is exercised only subject to the necessary restrictions imposed by laws and regulations, in particular in the interests of national security, the safety of others, health, morals or the rights and freedoms of individuals.

ARTICLE 12

1. Everyone has the right to freedom of movement and residence within a State, subject to compliance with the rules laid down by law.
2. Everyone has the right to leave any country, including his own, and to return to his country. This right may be subject to restrictions only if they are provided for by law, necessary to protect national security, public order, public health or morals.
3. Everyone has the right, in the event of persecution, to seek and receive asylum in foreign territory, in accordance with the law of each country and international conventions.
4. A foreigner lawfully admitted to the territory of a State party to the present Charter may be expelled from it only by a decision in accordance with the law.
5. The collective expulsion of foreigners is prohibited. Collective expulsion is the one that generally targets national, racial, ethnic or religious groups.

ARTICLE 13

1. All citizens have the right to participate freely in the conduct of the public affairs of their country, either directly or through freely chosen representatives, in accordance with the rules laid down by law.

2. All citizens also have the right to access public services in their country.
3. Everyone has the right to use public goods and services in strict equality before the law.

ARTICLE 14

The rights of ownership are guaranteed. They may only be affected by public necessity or in the general interest of the community, in accordance with the provisions of the appropriate laws.

ARTICLE 15

Everyone has the right to work under fair and satisfactory conditions and to receive equal pay for equal work.

ARTICLE 16

1. Everyone has the right to the enjoyment of the highest attainable standard of physical and mental health.
2. The States Parties to this Charter undertake to take the necessary measures to protect the health of their populations and to provide them with medical assistance in the event of illness.

ARTICLE 17

1. Everyone has the right to education.
2. Everyone may freely participate in the cultural life of the community.
3. The promotion and protection of morals and traditional values recognized by the community is a duty of the State in the context of the protection of human rights.

ARTICLE 18

1. The family is the natural and basic element of society. It must be protected by the State, which must ensure its physical and moral health.
2. The State has an obligation to assist the family in its mission as guardian of morals and traditional values recognized by the community.
3. The State has a duty to ensure the elimination of all discrimination against women and to ensure the protection of the rights of women and children as stipulated in international declarations and conventions.
4. Elderly or disabled persons are also entitled to specific protective measures in relation to their physical or moral needs.

ARTICLE 19

All peoples are equal; they enjoy the same dignity and have the same rights. Nothing can justify the domination of one people by another.

ARTICLE 20

1. Every people has the right to exist. Every people has an imprescriptible and inalienable right to self-determination. It freely determines its political status and ensures its economic and social development according to the path it has freely chosen.
2. Colonized or oppressed peoples have the right to free themselves from their state of domination by using all means recognized by the international community.
3. All peoples have the right to the assistance of the States Parties to the present Charter in their struggle for liberation from foreign domination, be it political, economic or cultural.

ARTICLE 21

1. The peoples have free access to their wealth and natural resources. This right is exercised in the exclusive interest of the populations. Under no circumstances can a people be deprived of it.
2. In the event of spoliation, the dispossessed peoples have the right to the legitimate recovery of their property and to adequate compensation.
3. The free disposal of natural wealth and resources shall be without prejudice to the obligation to promote international economic cooperation based on mutual respect, equitable exchange and the principles of international law.
4. . The States Parties to this Charter undertake, both individually and collectively, to exercise the right of free disposal of their natural wealth and resources, with a view to strengthening African unity and solidarity.
5. The States Parties to this Charter undertake to eliminate all forms of foreign economic exploitation, in particular that practised by international monopolies, in order to enable the population of each country to fully enjoy the benefits derived from its national resources.

ARTICLE 22

1. All peoples have the right to their economic, social and cultural development, with strict respect for their freedom and identity, and to the equal enjoyment of the common heritage of humanity.
2. States have a duty, individually or in cooperation, to ensure the exercise of the right to development.

ARTICLE 23

1. People have the right to peace and security both nationally and internationally. The principle of solidarity and friendly relations

implicitly affirmed by the Charter of the United Nations and reaffirmed by that of the Organization of African Unity in relations between States.
2. With the aim of strengthening peace, solidarity and friendly relations, the States Parties to this Charter undertake to prohibit:
   (a) a person enjoying the right of asylum under Article 12 of this Charter undertakes a subversive activity directed against his or her country of origin or against any other country party to this Charter;
   (b) their territories are used as a starting point for subversive or terrorist activities directed against the people of any other State party to this Charter.

ARTICLE 24

All peoples have the right to a satisfactory and global environment conducive to their development.

ARTICLE 25

States Parties to this Charter have a duty to promote and ensure, through education, and dissemination, respect for the rights and freedoms contained in this Charter, and to take measures to ensure that these freedoms and rights are understood and the corresponding obligations and duties.

ARTICLE 26

States Parties to this Charter have a duty to guarantee the independence of the courts and to allow the establishment and improvement of appropriate national institutions responsible for the promotion and protection of the rights and freedoms guaranteed by this Charter.

BOOK SUMMARY

"President Donald Trump hits the Africans" is a satirical, educational and revolutionary book. Indeed, he urges the Africans to change and rewrite their history. It pushes them to wake up, to abandon all their mortal defects (such as idiocy, laxity, unconsciousness, ignorance, torpor, corruption, selfishness, dishonesty, wickedness, lack of bravery) to embrace the virtues that have made the great Asian and Western nations or powers of today. He invites them to fight their pitiful, lamentable and revolting fate. It is a tool for the African renaissance and for the progress of Africans. He claims a new, better and dignified Africa based on solidarity, patriotism, humanism, responsibility.

ABOUT THE AUTHOR

François Adja Assemien was born in 1954 in Côte d'Ivoire (West Africa). He studied classic literature (French, Latin and Greek), human sciences and philosophy. He holds a PhD in philosophy and a Bachelor's degree in sociology, and has devoted himself to the teaching of philosophy, writing and academic research. He is the author of several published works (novels, essays, short stories, plays). He works on his own concepts such as Afrocratism, Philocure, Sidarology, Conscience Africaine, Phénoménologie de l'esprit et du comportement africains etc. He speaks and writes three modern languages: French, English and German.

www.ingramcontent.com/pod-product-compliance
Lightning Source LLC
LaVergne TN
LVHW091934070526
838200LV00068B/1222

Losing 100 pounds Naturally

Personal Insight from a Christian physician

Jean-Ronel Corbier, MD

© 2004 by Dr. Jean-Ronel Corbier. All rights reserved.

Printed in the United States of America

No part of this publication may be reproduced, stored in a retrieval system, or transmitted in any way by any means—electronic, mechanical, photocopy, recording, or otherwise—without the prior permission of the copyright holder, except as provided by USA copyright law.

Scripture references are taken from the King James Version of the Bible.

Scripture taken from the HOLY BIBLE, NEW INTERNATIONAL VERSION®. NIV®. Copyright©1973, 1978, 1984 by International Bible Society. Used by permission of Zondervan. All rights reserved.

Published by:
Ufomadu Consulting & Publishing
P.O. Box 746
Selma, AL 36702-0746

ISBN 0-9754197-5-7
Library of Congress Catalog Card Number: 2004195580